SAMUEL ADAMSON

Running Wild

an adaptation of the novel by
MICHAEL MORPURGO

D0718376

ff

FABER & FABER

First published in 2016
by Faber and Faber Limited
74–77 Great Russell Street
London WC1B 3DA

Typeset by Country Setting, Kingsdown, Kent CT14 8ES
Printed in England by CPI Group (UK) Ltd, Croydon CR0 4YY

A CIP record for this book
is available from the British Library

ISBN 978-0-571-33318-9

2 4 6 8 10 9 7 5 3

Adaptor's Notes

The stage version of *Running Wild* was made in two
separate productions by many people, including puppetry
designers and directors Finn Caldwell and Toby Olié for
Gyre & Gimble; Rod Paton, Paul Wills, Georgina Lamb,
Nick Powell, Paul Anderson, Nick Lidster, Andrew D
Edwards, Lizzi Gee, Oliver Kaderbhai and Kate Hunter;
the acting company at Regent's Park Theatre and members
of Chichester Festival Youth Theatre; and the directors,
Timothy Sheader and Dale Rooks. Many thanks to all of
them, and to Kathy Bourne and Michael Morpurgo.

Many of the stage directions in the text came before Dale
Rooks, Timothy Sheader and Gyre & Gimble's work.
They are not necessarily detailed (and never prescriptive)
where animal behaviour and communication are
concerned, and exist largely for general storytelling
shape. There are many stories to be told via the non-
verbal relationships between Lilly/Will and the animals,
and the animals and their environment.

Oona eats whatever and whenever she can.

Use music and song throughout, imaginatively and
liberally.

Chorus lines are broken by en dashes (–) to suggest
different groups or individuals; asterisked lines (*)
suggest full Chorus. But feel free to mash all this up.

Running Wild in this adaptation was first presented by Chichester Festival Youth Theatre at the Cass Sculpture Foundation, Goodwood, West Sussex, on 2 August 2015. The cast was as follows:

Will Alfie Scott
Dad Alex Wilcox
Mum Esme Cooper
Grandpa Rufus Cameron
Grandma Katie Morgan
Charlie Sacha Hemingway
Tonk Benjamin Mitchell
Mahout Jacob Thomas
Red Bandana Daniel Mears
Hunters Tommy Dew, Jay Dix, Ben Hughes
    Lindon Jones, Alex Wilcox
Kaya Tom Chown
Mr Anthony Rufus Cameron
Dr Geraldine Gemma Sangster

Puppeteers
Kingfisher Luc Garner-Gibbons
Oona Harrison De Bathe, Emily Dyble, Sami Green,
    Nicholas Jacobs, Liam Wright
Tiger Darcy Collins, Susie Coutts, Charlie Daniells
Mani Fred Davis, Romina Hytten
'Charlie' Freya Peake
'Tonk' William Browne

Chorus
  Nathan Arbuckle, Georgia Ashman, Ella Bassett-Jull,
  Kate Bolton, William Browne, Richard Chapman,
  Tom Chown, Darcy Collins, Esme Cooper, Susie Coutts,
  Cameron Cragg, Benjamin Cranny Whitehead,
  Zoe Crisp, Charlie Daniells, Joy-Beth Davey, Georgia
  Dearnley, Eleanor Dickens, Heather Falconer, Luc
  Garner-Gibbons, Jennifer Goodier, Sacha Hemingway,
  Ella Heryet, Ben Hughes, Alyssia Jansz, Francesca Key,
  Amy Kirkman, India Loseby, Jude Loseby, Thomas
  Lunn, Polly Maltby, Emily Mcalpine, Marc Mcgee-
  Russell, Olivia Mcgurk, Benjamin Mitchell, Katie
  Morgan, Ella O'Keeffe, Megan O'Neill, George
  Orchard, Katie Owen, Freya Peake, Ellie Phelan, Lucy
  Pratt, Gemma Sangster, Josie Smith, Martha Swain,
  Scarlett Taylor-Jones, Jacob Thomas, Sophie Turner,
  George Waller, Maddison Wedge, Claudia White

Director Dale Rooks
Puppetry Design and Direction Finn Caldwell
  and Toby Olié, for Gyre & Gimble
Designer Andrew D. Edwards
Movement Lizzi Gee
Music Rod Paton
Assistant Director Kate Hunter

Running Wild in a co-production by Regent's Park Theatre and Chichester Festival Theatre was first presented at the Regent's Park Open Air Theatre, London, on 13 May 2016. The cast was as follows:

Will	Will	Lilly
Joshua Fernandes	Tyler Osborne	Ava Potter

Dad Ira Mandela Siobhan
Mum Hattie Ladbury
Granny Joyce Henderson
Grandad Eric Mallett
Oona, *an elephant*
  Laura Cubitt (*trunk*), Ben Thompson (*head*)
  Michael Taibi (*heart*), John Leader (*hind*)
Mahout Okorie Chukwu
Mani, *an orang-utan*
  Stuart Angell (*head*), Sarah Mardel (*body*)
'Charlie', *an orang-utan* Romina Hytten
'Tonk', *an orang-utan* Fred Davis
Red Bandana Okorie Chukwu
Hunter Ira Mandela Siobhan
Mr Anthony Stephen Ventura
Kaya Eric Mallett
Dr Geraldine Hattie Ladbury

Other characters and animals played by members of the Company.

Young People's Ensemble
  Rochelle Addo, Megan Allen, Lauryn Alleyne,
  Esme Anderson, Salima Benslika Ruiz, Ella Bernstein,

Lucy Bernstein, Destinée Bishop, Henrietta Charnley,
Darcy Collins, Charlie Daniells, Annabelle Dennis,
Nell Dobson, Ranya Dool, Emily Dyble, Alex Eden,
Daniel Edo Ukeh, Kira Elderfield-Tuitt, Gina Fasseland,
Jodi Flinn, Marco Foster, Hannah Grange, Fatima
Hussain, Oumar Jah, Lauryn Jenkins, Kate Kamgshuva,
Thomas King, Kate Kirpichenko, Faithful Lawson,
Noah Leigh, Noga Levy-Rappaport, Alex McCaragher,
Emile McDonald, Clara Mello, Beauty Odeyemi,
Sima Ogden, Nora Omar Arbe, Jackson O'Neill,
Denise Parente, Amelia Phillips, Alicia Poon, Christian
Powlesland, Costanza Pucci, Mariam Raidi, Nico
Saggese, Salma Sajil, Ann Marie Scally, Yinka Shokunbi,
Tim Siddique, Victoria Sinel, Sarah Soliman, Nathan
Tadesse, Angela Tavares, Millie Turner

Directors Timothy Sheader and Dale Rooks
Designer Paul Wills
Puppetry Design and Direction Finn Caldwell
    and Toby Olié, for Gyre & Gimble
Movement Director Georgina Lamb
Original Music/Composer Rod Paton
Sound Score Nick Powell
Lighting Designer Paul Anderson
Sound Designer Nick Lidster for Autograph
Season Associate Director (*Voice and Text*)
    Barbara Houseman
Casting Director Jessica Ronane CDG
Ensemble Casting Verity Naughton
Music Director Louise Duggan
Assistant Director Oliver Kaderbhai

Characters

The central character can be a girl or a boy. If she's a girl, her name is Lilly (shortened to Lil for 'Chill, Lil' and 'Where there's a Lil there's a way'). If a boy, his name is Will. For simplicity's sake (and because he is a boy in Michael Morpurgo's original novel) the character is referred to as Will in the following text. If the character is a girl, replace 'Will' with 'Lilly' or 'Lil' throughout, and alter all applicable personal pronouns, etc.

IN INDONESIA

Mahout
an elephant handler

Red Bandana
a hunter

Kaya
a chef

Mr Anthony
an Australian palm oil king

Dr Geraldine

IN ADDITION

Chorus
of singers and storytellers, with as many
young people in it as possible, who play:
Football Supporters/Friends of Will's, in England
Soldiers/Mourners, in England
Animal and Element Puppeteers, throughout
Swimmers, at the Indonesian beach
Hunters, in the rainforest
Workers, at Mr Anthony's
Bodyguards, to Mr Anthony
Foster Mothers, to baby orang-utans in the sanctuary

ANIMALS

Oona
elephant

Tiger

Crocodile

Orang-utans
including

Mani
dark-haired female orang-utan, mother to 'Charlie'

'Charlie'
baby female orang-utan

'Tonk'
baby male orang-utan

Others wherever and whenever possible
in the rainforest such as:

Butterflies, Insects, Snakes,
Birds (Toucans, Kingfishers, Peacocks etc.),
Fish, Gibbons, Monkeys, Bats

RUNNING WILD

This text is for Dale Rooks

Act One

*The Chorus ignites the story. All carry Manchester
United FC flags and sing the Manchester United song.*

Chorus
Glory, glory, Man United,
Glory, glory, Man United,
Glory, glory, Man United,
As the Reds go marching
On! On! On!

*Will breaks from the crowd. He is wearing a
Manchester United scarf.*

Yesss!

Will Goal! Two–nil, Dad, we're thrashing them!

Dad appears.

Dad (*sings*)
Wem-ber-ly! Wem-ber-ly!

Will *and* **Dad**
We're the famous Man United
And we're going to Wem-ber-ly!

Dad (*offers chips*) Chips – with vinegar. Your favourite.

Will (*stuffs face excitedly*) Yeah, but this isn't all we're
going to eat, we have to have a pie, whenever we're at
Old Trafford, we eat pies.

Dad And I won't tell Mum if you don't.

Will I don't want today to end, Dad.

A controversial tackle: they react.

3

Let's not go back to Salisbury.

Dad What are you on about?

Will It's really boring, and it's not your proper home, that's Granny and Grandad's farm – why can't we live there? I want to be there with all the animals.

Dad But Granny and Grandad's doesn't have your favourite animal, does it?

Will No. Because there are no elephants in Yorkshire.

Dad And have you heard the one about why?

Will Yes, a million times –

Dad There's this boy, his name's, um, Will, and he's on the train to his grandparents' farm, and this nutcase bloke, let's call him Dad, has a Sainsbury's bag full of bananas. But instead of eating them, every few minutes this dad throws one out the window. And Will thinks this is weird and says, 'Why are you throwing your bananas away?' And Dad says, 'To keep the elephants away. 'Cause elephants are dangerous, they charge at trains.' And Will says, 'But this is Yorkshire, there are no stampeding elephants in Yorkshire.' And Dad says, 'That's right, there aren't –'

He pantomimes lobbing a banana out a window.

'– 'cause they're too busy eating my bananas.'

He laughs at his own joke, tackles or tickles Will.

Will You think you're so funny – Get off!

The possibility of a goal. The sounds of the football ground diminish. The natural world makes its music.

Dad Here's a real story about elephants. Some people think that when they reach a certain age, they know they're going to die. They just feel in their bones that their time's come. So they leave their group and go off by themselves.

4

Will I wish *your* proper time had come, Dad.

Dad It did.

Will No. I want to drive the tractor and go lambing at Granny and Grandad's like we used to – go camping – Remember when we saw a kingfisher – and the nature programmes we used to watch –

Dad You've got your mum . . .

Will But it doesn't feel like our family any more –

Dad Don't say that. When she was your age, she came here from halfway across the world – think about that. Chill, Will. Where there's a Will there's a way, eh?

Will But, Dad, remember how we used to go fishing –

Beret-wearing soldiers appear, bearing a flag-covered coffin. They are followed in procession by mourners including Mum, Granny, Grandad and Will's friends Charlie (who in sympathy with Will wears a Manchester United scarf) and Tonk (who is in Chelsea FC blue: a scarf and a shirt; she has a football). All sing a hymn, 'The Day Thou Gavest'.

(*To Dad.*) – and the Rudyard Kipling stories you'd read to me. How the elephant got its trunk?

Dad You just have to keep going, Will.

He sings the Manchester United song as he retreats and disappears: it sounds discordant against the hymn. Will tries to follow, but he is engulfed by the funeral.

Will (*overlapping*) Dad? Dad! Come back! Dad!

Mum tries to grab him. He breaks from her. He runs and runs. The funeral scatters and Charlie and Tonk chase after him. And . . .

SCENE TWO
WILL'S FRIENDS

In a new place, Will stops running, out of breath.

Will Dad? Dad? Where are you? . . .

   Charlie and Tonk catch up with him.

Charlie Will!

Will Did you see him? . . .

Charlie Who?

Will We were watching football – everything was red . . .

Tonk Oh, yeah, everything's red. (*Re her Chelsea kit.*)
Sorry – I know today's about you, but I wouldn't live it
down if I even *touched* a Man U shirt.

Charlie (*under his breath*) Tonk.

Tonk (*under hers*) What?

Will I'm going.

Charlie Where?

Will Yorkshire.

Tonk What? How?

Will I'm walking.

Charlie Wait! Your grandad's looking for you, everyone's
going back to yours for cake. It was nice . . . I've never
seen so many people at church.

Tonk You can bunk off school for months now.

Charlie Tonk.

Tonk What? (*To Will*.) He was a hero, your dad.

She plays football around him.

. . . And it's Francesca Lampard on the ball, and she sees Rio Ferdinand, ten seconds left and she goes past Ferdinand like a knife through butter and she –

She kicks, magnificently – the glory!

What a goal! Forty thousand Chelsea fans go wild –

She taunts Will with her Chelsea scarf.

– and Man U are devastated!

Charlie Tonk.

Tonk What, Charlie? (*To Will*.) Hey – why don't they drink tea in Manchester? 'Cause all the cups are at Stamford Bridge.

Charlie (*to Will*) Let's go.

Will Why? There's nothing at home.

Tonk You can't walk all the way from Salisbury to Yorkshire.

Will Watch me.

He runs off.

Charlie Will! (*To Tonk*.) Nice one.

Tonk You're the one who's weird with him, Charlie. Act normal.

Charlie Oh, because your dad driving over a bomb in the middle of Iraq is 'normal', is it?

Tonk I've got no idea what to say to him, but you don't either.

Charlie We'd better stop him.

He and Tonk run off after Will as Mum and Granny are seen . . .

Will!

Tonk Will!

SCENE THREE
TO INDONESIA

In Mum's home.

Granny Grandad will find him – he always does.

Mum Why does he keep doing this?

Granny He's not going to stop asking, you know.

Mum We can't just live with you – my work's here, his school – (*Snaps.*) God, what was Chris thinking? I mean it: why did he have to join up only to get himself killed?

This is upsetting to both of them.

I'm sorry . . . I loved Chris . . . and I know I shouldn't be angry . . . but you shouldn't have lost a son, he shouldn't have lost a father, and I shouldn't have to pretend I'm coping when I'm not. His dad's not in Yorkshire, he's gone, he's gone, and I just want to squeeze all the pain out of Will . . .

Grandad and Will appear.

Grandad Here he is.

Mum Will! Where have you been?

Grandad He just needed a bit of fresh air.

Mum I've told you: you have to stay with me.

Will I didn't want to see all those people.

Granny Don't worry, we've cancelled – so we have lots of cake to eat now.

Will When are you going back to Yorkshire, Granny? Grandad said to ask you.

Granny Don't worry about that. We're staying here for a bit to help your mum . . .

Will But when you go, can I come with you?

A moment.

Granny A nice piece of Victoria sponge, that'll do the trick.

Will I'm not hungry.

Granny Yes you are, and you'll eat it all up like a good boy.

Will I said I'm not hungry.

He charges out. Mum follows.

Mum Will –!

Will goes to his own room, still visible; he finds a Rudyard Kipling book with a photo inside; he stares at it and hums or sings the Manchester United song. Mum pauses near the door.

Will Everyone's acting weird, Dad. Granny just bakes cakes, Grandad doesn't say anything, Charlie and Tonk say too much. It's like I don't belong any more – at least in Yorkshire I could get lost in the wild world . . .

Mum returns to the other room. Grandad has been sitting silently; Granny has been busying herself.

Granny All right?

Mum Not really. I wish I knew what to do.

Granny Maya . . . I don't want you to live with us. What I mean is . . . I'd love to have him, but you're right, what would it solve? We can't fix things for ourselves, let alone him. We don't need to think about any of that now – I wasn't going to do this today, but . . .

She shows her a brochure. Mum is confused by it.

I picked it up in town yesterday. We'd pay.

Mum What?

Granny (*to Grandad*) We've got a little money put aside, haven't we?

Mum Are you mad?

Granny I mean for both of you.

Mum But . . . we can't just go to the other side of the world . . .

Granny Not for good – for Christmas. You should show Will where *your* father came from. He knows England and our heritage – what about yours? This could be the time to discover all that. See . . . the beach . . . palm trees . . . and look, his favourite. (*To Grandad.*) You agree, don't you?

Grandad I'll miss him . . . Whatever's best.

Granny Perhaps it would help to put things back together for him, somehow.

Mum I can barely put one foot in front of the other –

Granny Just think about it.

She presses the brochure into Mum's hand and leaves. Mum goes to Will's room.

Mum Will?

She sits by him.

Will Why did he have to go, Mum?

Mum He was a soldier. Soldiers fight, you know that.

Will I know I know that, Dad told me that, but why won't anyone tell me what the war's for, what's it actually *for*?

She can't answer.

You never answer my questions. He said it was the last time he was going –

Mum And it was – it was –

Will You promised me when he left that he'd come back!

Mum Shhh . . .

She tries to comfort him. She takes his book.

'The Elephant's Child'. I don't think you'll ever grow out of this. (*She reads.*) 'In the Far-Off Times, the Elephant had no trunk, but a bulgy nose, as big as a boot. But there was one Elephant, an Elephant's Child . . .'

Will isn't listening – but he has discovered the travel brochure. He is instantly captivated.

I know I'm not the reader Dad was . . .

Will (*re something in the brochure; he can't take his eyes off it*) Look.

Mum Oh . . . yes . . . it's, um . . . an idea of Granny's . . . I don't think it's a very sensible idea, really, but . . .

Will Indonesia . . . !

The Chorus sings. The sea is seen. A moment. Mum sees something new in Will: she is amazed by his engagement.

Mum Would you like to go?

He is too busy devouring the brochure to answer.

It's a very long flight . . . and we'd need malaria injections . . . and we'd miss Christmas Day with Granny and Grandad . . . and Boxing Day with your cousins . . . and –

Will (*turns a page, points and sees something very exciting*) Look!

Mum Yes. They have them there. You really want to do this?

Will stands eagerly, clutching the brochure.

Will Granny!

Mum Will?

He rushes off, shouting. The Chorus's song builds.

Will Grandad!

Mum All right, Will.

Chorus (*as required*)
– The sea, the sea,
– the ocean,
– the murmuring Indian Ocean . . .

Mum runs towards the sea, shouting joyfully at the view. She changes, before us, into a sarong. The Chorus as swimmers are seen on the beach and in the water.

Mum Will! Look, look at it gleaming!

Chorus
The shimmering sea, the sea,
– the ocean,
– *the whispering Indian Ocean . . .

Mum The blue . . . I'd forgotten it . . . and the whiteness of the sand . . .

Chorus
  – The soft and silent sand
  – of the pristine beach, the beach,
  – *the Indonesian beach.

Mum It's like a dream. It's home, really . . .

She looks off towards Will, and laughs.

Will (*off*) Mum, look!

Mum You're on top! You're on top, on top –

SCENE FOUR
WILL MEETS OONA

Will appears magnificently out of the trees, wearing shorts, Manchester United T-shirt and hat, and sitting on a beautiful elephant, Oona, who trumpets as he screams.

Will – On top of the world!

Oona is led by a Mahout, who wears a long white shirt. They walk along the beach. Throughout, Oona keeps trying to wrap her trunk around the Mahout's shirt, and he speaks to her in confidential whispers. The swimmers remain.

Mum Hold on!

Will Thank you, Mum, thank you!

Mum Don't fall off! – Wait, I have to get this on video –

Will I never thought this would happen to me, ever –

Mum Show Granny and Grandad your smile!

Will Hi, Granny, hi, Grandad, it's Will here on a massive *elephant*, ten times the size of one of your cows, isn't he amazing?

Mahout He's not a he, he's a she. Called Oona.

Will Oona? Hello, Oona, I'm Will from England. And you're so beautiful – look at all the colours in your skin –

Mum Some of it's almost pink. A pink elephant.

Will How old is she, Mr Mahout?

Mahout Twelve. I've known her since she was born, she's like a sister to me.

Mahout whispers to Oona. Will hugs her neck and chats to her himself.

Mum I wonder what he's whispering? You sure you're all right up there?

Will Yes, Mum.

Mum (*to Mahout*) He is safe?

Mahout Yes, Oona likes people. She's very friendly and very intelligent.

Mum I'd hate you to fall.

Will Mum?

Mum What?

Will Do you like swimming?

Mum Yes. Why?

Will *Go swimming.*

Mum Are you trying to get rid of me? (*In Indonesian.*) He's trying to get rid of me.

Mahout (*in Indonesian*) You speak Indonesian?

Mum (*in Indonesian*) A little.

Will What are you saying?

Mum (*to Will*) So I can leave you, your majesty?

Will I'm fine!

Mum I don't want you getting sunburnt: keep your shirt and hat on.

Will Yes, Mum.

Mum And drink this!

She throws a bottle of water up to him.

Will Yes, Mum.

Mum And put more of that sunscreen on.

Will Yes, Mum.

Mum So I'll see you when I get back?

Mahout Yes, Mum.

Mum is suddenly overwhelmed.

Will What's the matter? – Don't cry.

Mum It's just I haven't seen you this happy for so long.

Will Because everything's all right now. This is the best Christmas present ever. I'm king of the world!

He punches the air, whooshes with joy. Mum leaves for the distant swimmers and melts into the water. Oona walks.

SCENE FIVE
TSUNAMI

Mahout Your mother's Indonesian?

Will Half. So I'm quarter.

Mahout Your first time here? Your dad is with you?

Will Look how the rainforest disappears into the clouds. What a view you're giving me, Oona – you're so gentle and good.

Mahout Good? Her? Naughty. I didn't tell your mother this. Very naughty sometimes – if she wants to run, I can't stop her. And it's a strange thing, today I think she's not feeling so good.

Will She's sick?

Mahout This morning I took her to the sea for her swim and she didn't want to go in. She loves the sea, but she stood looking out as if she'd never seen it before. One thing I know for sure: you can't make Oona do what Oona doesn't want to do.

Will Perhaps she's hungry.

Oona trumpets. Mahout whispers to her. Will hugs her neck and chats to her himself.

I'm going to ride you again tomorrow, Oona, and I'll bring bananas. Because you make me feel like I'm floating miles above everything sad. How are you so gentle when you're so huge, have you got shock-absorbers in your feet? Huh, look: a plane! I was up there like that and there was an elephant just like you in Granny's holiday brochure, maybe it *was* you, and now we're together, isn't that incredible?

Mahout She's happier now. I think it's because she likes you. She'll never let you fall. I can tell this when I look in her eyes.

Will Her eyes?

Mahout It's how elephants speak, with their eyes.

Will Truly?

Mahout Truly. She tells me she's at peace.

Will So, Oona, did you hear the one about why there are no elephants in Devon? There's this boy, and his name's, um, Will, and –

Oona stops walking. Mahout looks out to sea.

Chorus
- – The sea, the ocean,
- – *the Indian Ocean
- – is still.

Oona breathes short, sharp breaths. Throughout the next Mahout whispers at her.

Mahout Oona –?

Will It's like a mill pond out there. So, there's this nutcase dad and they're on a train and he has a Sainsbury's bag full of bananas –

Mahout You want to go back? –

Will Back? No! Can't we go a bit further? You'll be around tomorrow won't you, Mr Mahout?

Mahout Oona –

Will Mr Mahout?

Mahout is anxious. Will looks back to where they've come from.

Where's Mum? I can't see her. Mr Mahout, which one's our hotel?

Mahout The white roof. Come on, Oona –

Will They're all white. She's wearing . . . I can't remember . . . is she swimming? I think her bikini's red . . . or blue . . .

Mahout Oona, move –

Chorus
- – The sea, the ocean,
- – *the Indian ocean,
- – is waiting,

- *waiting, waiting, waiting,
- waiting, waiting, waiting,
- waiting, waiting, waiting,
- waiting . . .

Will What's wrong with her? Is everything OK? I think we should go back to Mum – I can't see Mum –

Mahout Come on, Oona, for God's sake, move! –

Oona lifts her trunk, tosses her head, trumpets at the sea, terrified.

Mahout Calm down . . . calm down, girl . . . shhhh . . .

Silence.

Will Look.

Mahout is motionless, dumbstruck. As are the distant swimmers. The sea is sucked away – the water disappears. Thousands of fish flounder on the sand.

Mum?

Swimmers rush forward joyfully to grab the fish.

Mum?

Rumbling.

What's that?

Suddenly Oona bolts into the trees with Will still on her back.

Mahout Oona! (*In Indonesian.*) Stop, Oona!

Will Mum! Mum! Mum!

And now the sea returns – as a giant wave. The swimmers scream and yell, ad lib, some in Indonesian, all building to a fever pitch:

Swimmers Mum! – Akmal! – Claudia! – Dad! – Auntie Sarah! – Stefan! – Run! – Lia, Lia! – Oh, my God. – What is that? – That man doesn't realise! – Help! – Granny! – What's happening? – Quickly!

Mahout Oona! Stop! Oona!

Mum Will! Will! Help! Where are you?

Will Mum! Mum! Muuuuuum!

The sea surges, the wave is colossal. And . . .

Devastation. The swimmers, Mum and Mahout have gone, drowned, and Will and Oona have disappeared. Terrible silence. The Chorus sings. And . . .

SCENE SIX
TO THE RAINFOREST

Oona charges towards, then through the rainforest. Will loses his water bottle. Time passes, the landscape and conditions change:

Will Oona . . . Ooona, nooo, go back, please! That couldn't have been the ocean, it's impossible! Mum. Mum! Oona, you have to turn around! I have to go back! Turn around, Ooona! Muuuum! *etc., ad lib.*

Chorus (*as required*)
    – She knows,
    – the wave, the terror,
    – the dread, the screams,
    – *she knows,
    – the column of green, the wave
    – the tremor, the throb,
    – *the forest,
    – the forest,
    – the dark, the rush,
    – the torrent,
    – the storm,
    – *tsunami . . .*

Will God, Oona, how? Go back, go back . . .

Chorus
- – The shadows,
- – the trees,
- – *the scrub, the drone,
- – the branches,
- – whip, gash,
- – lash, claw,
- – the rocks, the wet,
- – the mud, the mire, the swamp,
- – *the swamp, the horror, the screams,
- – the stench, the blood,
- – *the day, night,
- – soaked, bruised,
- – cut, confused . . .

Will hears a sound overhead; he looks up, shouts, flails his arms.

Will Helicopter! Hello! Down here! Help! SOS!

Rain. Hail.

Oona, she's still alive. She didn't go swimming, she hated water. She went back to the hotel, our room was on the top floor, she would have been safe. Because how could the ocean go so high?

Chorus
- – *Breathe,
- – breathe,
- – the clearing,
- – the sky,
- – the grass, the flies,
- – the feed,
- – *the leaves,
- – the stream, the peace,
- – *the feed, feed.

Will She's emailing Grandad. She's definitely in the hotel, we have to go back. Oona! Please. Mum, don't give up.

Chorus
- – The breeze,
- – the day, the night, the light,
- – *the day, the light,
- – the loss, the hope,
- – *the loss.

Oona sleeps, standing.

Will Where's my water bottle . . . ? Mum . . . Mum . . . Mum . . . I'm going to die . . . Someone . . . What am I going to do?

He clutches Oona's neck, sobbing. He sleeps. The Chorus sings and . . .

SCENE SEVEN
TIGER

The Jungle comes to life. All the sounds: the full orchestra of it, animals, birds and insects singing, shrieking, buzzing. There is danger for the sleeping Will – what is it? – a Tiger! Birds fly off, Oona is disturbed. Will wakes, and . . .

SCENE EIGHT
FRIENDS AND THIRST

Will Mum!

Mum appears. Oona eats leaves.

Mum? It was a dream . . .

Mum You've been in and out of sleep for days.

Will I'm boiling. I'm thirsty. I'm drenched –

Mum It's a rainforest. It rains.

Will – It came so fast, it wasn't real, like some computer game, and when I looked back I saw girls clinging to trees, and cars floating like toys, and the screaming, crying, the whole seafront was gone and it swallowed our hotel, and Oona was going faster up the hill and we were leaving you –

Mum She felt the danger in her bones.

Will But you love swimming, you're strong, you can outswim anything –

Mum Not an earthquake under the sea.

Will Mum, let's go home now, remember how we used to pretend to eat Granny's Victoria sponge and secretly feed it to the dog –

Jungle music. Mum retreats and disappears.

Mum? Mum, don't drown –

He cries, terrified. Screeching. He sings to find his courage.

Glory, glory, Man United,
Glory, glory, Man United . . .

Oona puts her trunk up and touches Will. She feels his face. At last he comprehends exactly what she has done.

Oona . . . Oona, it was thanks to you. Because you ran, we've got this far. You saved my life, I wouldn't have stood a chance. All those people . . . none of them could have survived that . . . and you just knew . . . Mum . . . she could be alive, yes? I don't know . . . I don't think *you* think so . . . there couldn't possibly be anyone alive down there . . . you knew the jungle is where we'd be safe. Thank you, Oona, thank you, you're my friend . . .

He hugs her, then finds himself laughing through his tears at Oona's trunk.

That tickles –

Oona's breath is bad and he gags. He smells his own breath.

– and your breath's disgusting . . . Ew, so is mine. We can have dog breath together. Together.

He slaps an insect. Oona eats.

Because except for these blood-sucking leeches . . . and God knows what else . . . it's just you and me –

Screeching.

Chill, Will, that's what Dad used to say. 'Where there's a Will, there's a way.' I'll get back to the coast to find Mum. I'm not alone. You saved my life, Oona, so I'm not going to lose it now – which means . . . drink . . .

Oona walks.

Wem-ber-ly, Wem-ber-ly . . .

I'm thirsty. Oona? Do you understand? Drink.

He slaps Oona's neck, he drowses.

We're the famous Will and Oona
And we're going to Wem-ber-ly . . .

I really, really need water, Oona, my throat's burning . . .

Oona just walks, and eats. In his delirium, Will improvises new words for the song.

Need to drink, need to drink,
We're the thirsty Will and Oona
And I really need to . . .

He falls asleep and . . .

SCENE NINE
THE RIVER AND CROCODILE

They arrive at a river. The Chorus sings. Oona enters the water and drinks with no concern for Will. Will wakes.

Will Oona? At last! . . . Hey, that's not fair, what about me? Oona, I have to drink too . . .

He's desperate, frustrated.

Come on then, Will . . . you can do it . . . how cold can it be? Ten . . . nine . . . one –

He slides/falls/jumps off Oona. He screams as he hits the cold water. He drinks.

God, it never tasted so good!

Playtime: Oona squirts water at him.

Oi!

He squirts water back. He laughs, swims, chants. (During the next, Oona disappears down the river. Will doesn't realise that she seems to be leaving him.)

'There's only one David Beckham! One David Beckham, there's only –!'

Rubbish floats down the river – plastic bottles, clothing, etc. More frightening than this: a crocodile is in the water. It circles Will; he doesn't realise.

No way? Rubbish all the way out *here*? Hey, this could be handy –

He collects and holds something up – it's a Chelsea FC long-sleeve jersey.

Chelsea?! – you're kidding me, Tonk?! I'll never live this down . . . I've just had a brainwave: I could fish!

He gets out of the river with the jersey. Something occurs to him about it: it gives him pause.

Wait . . . this could've belonged to someone caught in the wave.

He looks back to the river. He has to survive.

I'm not relying on you for water again, Oona, I'm having that bottle.

He attempts to retrieve a water bottle before it floats away. The Crocodile attacks. He is lucky to escape with his life. He scrambles to the shore. He runs.

Oona? Oona, where are you? Oooona?

And . . .

SCENE TEN
ABANDONMENT

Will is wet, shivering with cold.

Will Come back, please . . . don't leave me . . . Oona . . . Oona, I'm freezing . . .

Sudden movement in the trees. It's a dark-haired orang-utan (referred to here by her eventual name: Mani). She terrifies him – he doesn't see her.

I'm not scared . . .

Sudden and alarming claps of thunder. Will doesn't know which way to go. He trembles, holds back tears.

I'm not feeling sorry for myself . . . I can survive this . . . I don't need an elephant.

But he does, and he cries.

Come back, Oona . . . please . . .

Oona saunters on indifferently, eating as always.

Oona!

He rushes to her, then plays it cool.

Yeah, well, I knew you'd miss me . . .

Oona farts. Will laughs, grimaces. He hugs her. Oona just wants to eat.

I'm sorry, I should've trusted you – it was jungle hide-and-seek, wasn't it?

He is overjoyed, the relief overwhelming.

The Chorus sings as something beautiful appears: a kaleidoscope of butterflies, flapping and floating all around.

Wow. Mum and Dad would have loved this.

He understands something new.

Except . . . I'm here with you . . . *you're* the one I need now. As long as we're together, I'll be OK. Maybe one day you'll carry me out of this jungle like you carried me in – but till then I'll survive because of you.

Oona just eats. Will is suddenly and painfully aware of his own hunger.

But only if I get something to eat too. I can't believe I'm craving Victoria sponge. Oona – I might die.

The Chorus sings. Oona walks and eats; Will trudges after her, increasingly weak. Time passes and the landscape changes . . .

Listen to me . . . please . . .

And . . .

SCENE ELEVEN
HUNGER

Will is sick with hunger. He tries everything.

Will . . . This can't go on. (*Angry.*) How much more can you rub my nose in it, munching and rumbling? We have to go where there's food for me, how do I ride you again, you stupid fat Jabba the Hut! (*Cajoling.*) Sweet Oona, jubbly elephant, take me where there's an ickle bite to eat? (*Begging.*) Pleeaaasseee, the tummy pangs, why did you save me if you're just going to let me dieee?

He grabs a leafy branch and pretends to eat, demonstrating to her. He points to his mouth, rubs his stomach, etc.

Aaahhh. ('*Delicious*' *with sibilance, like Kaa in* The Jungle Book) Dee-liss-see-awss food for Will the man-cub, yum-yum-nosh-nosh.

Oona eats the leaves herself. He whacks her, and hurts himself in the process.

Ouch! –

Suddenly, he sees something up high.

There! Is that some kind of fruit? This way, over here. Let me ride you! I can't reach it, Oona, I can't reach –

He tries to climb on Oona but fails. He tries to climb up the tree but there's nothing to cling to, and he is dizzy. Oona just eats. He is defeated, helpless; he buries his face in his hands, muttering and crying. Dad appears.

Chill, Will; chill, Will; chill, Will . . . I can't remember how I got up on her.

Dad How did the Mahout speak to her?

Will I don't know.

Dad You do.

Will He whispered.

Dad He told you: 'Elephants speak with their eyes.'

Will approaches Oona and whispers to her, staring into her eyes. She stops eating, stares.

Will You understand.

But nothing happens. He loses his temper again.

Suit yourself.

He walks off. He has nearly disappeared when the Chorus makes its Jungle Music, gentle, beautiful, magical, as Oona groans, kneels and reaches out her trunk. Will stops, his back to her.

Dad You have an invitation.

Will turns. He dares to smile, and walks to Oona gingerly. She curls her trunk around him, draws him in, nudges, lifts. He clambers until he is astride her neck. She heaves herself up and the music builds.

Will Woah . . . Top of the world . . .

And now he can reach the trees with the fruit, and Oona reaches with her trunk.

They're figs . . . figs, Oona . . . figs!

He stuffs his face. Dad disappears.

Thank you, thank you . . . This is better than chips with vinegar at Old Trafford with Dad! I love you, Oona. I love you so much.

Oona farts.

Stop farting!

He laughs. He improvises on their Manchester United song again as they head off.

Coconuts! Coconuts!
Now I've stuffed my face with figs
We need to find some coconuts! . . .

Mani appears, curious. She follows them. And . . .

SCENE TWELVE
FISHING AND MANI

A stream is seen. Fish are in it.

Will runs on, dirtier and wilder than he was, holding the Chelsea jersey. Time has passed. Ingeniously, the jersey has been fashioned into a fishing net: the arms are tied together and the bottom has been threaded on to bendy sticks and attached to lengths of jungle twine. Thus when pulled by the twine through the water, the jersey balloons to form a trap.

Will Morning, Oona!

Oona ambles on. Will chatters as he makes a final adjustment to the net.

Did I ever tell you the story of how you got your trunk by Rudyard Kipling? You said to your mum, 'I'm going to the grey-green greasy Limpopo River to see what the Crocodile has for dinner,' and your mum spanked you. To be continued. First, Exhibit A: my new trawling net, otherwise known as the useless Chelsea goalkeeper. Exhibit B: fish in the stream that go by the name of Fishy Wayne Rooney.

He wades into the stream and pulls the Chelsea net by the jungle twine. Fish swim past him and past the net. Will commentates.

And he's in there, his eye's on the back of the net . . .
loser! Come on . . . Fishy Rooney's been on good form
this season, it's an open goal . . . and he misses, the
shame! Go on, go on, my son, they think it's all over . . .
it is now!

*He swoops the 'net' out of the water and grabs his
catch.*

Lunch.

He kills and scales the fish with a rock.

You know, Oona, I think I've realised something . . .
I don't think there's much point trying to find a way
back . . . you're all the friend I need. All that matters is
we stick to our plan to stay alive for now. This is our life.
We're wild.

He eats the fish.

So, How You Got Your Trunk, Chapter Two. On your
way to the Crocodile's, you met a Bi-Coloured-Python-
Rock-Snake and you said, "Scuse me, but have you seen
a crocodile in these promiscuous parts?'

He notices Mani. She might be attracted by the food.

Oh, hello. What's your game, orang-utan, are you
following us? Don't think I haven't seen you, watching me.

They regard each other.

Whoever you are . . . you're beautiful.

Oona makes her presence felt.

Yes, Oona, you're beautiful too.

Suddenly:

SCENE THIRTEEN
TIGER TWO

The Chorus sings. A hullabaloo of alarm. Mani runs off, crashing through the trees. Oona is on edge.

Will Oona?

> *The Tiger appears. S/he hisses. Oona trumpets, raises her trunk, displays ears. The Tiger stalks Will. S/he comes very close. Oona protects him. It's a very dangerous encounter. Shielded by Oona, amazed by the Tiger's beauty, Will recites a poem: it seems to whisper through the rainforest – the Chorus echoes the words.*

> Tyger Tyger, burning bright,
> In the forests of the night;
> What immortal hand or eye,
> Dare frame thy fearful symmetry?

> *Oona tosses her head, swings her trunk, swishes her tail. The Tiger hisses, bares her/his teeth, twitches his/her tail. Standoff. The Tiger disappears.*

Oona . . . you did it . . . you just faced down the biggest killing machine in the world. You're the smartest, coolest elephant, the Queen of the Jungle. Oh, but he was beautiful. I've never seen anything like him. That poem from school . . . it just came into my head . . . We'll keep our distance if we see him again . . . everything has its place . . . feel it coming . . . be safe not sorry . . . but, oh, I hope he comes again!

> *The Chorus sings as Will climbs on Oona.*

So, Oona, you were walking along the Limpopo River . . .

> *Oona trumpets. She journeys as her rider natters.*

Yes, I know you've heard it a million times, so what? You trod on a log but it was the Crocodile and he caught you by your nose and you pulled and it grew longer and it hurt you hideous and *that's* how you got your trunk the end.

He sleeps on the journey. During the song, figs fall from the trees, and . . .

SCENE FOURTEEN
PARADISE

Mani reappears. This time she has a baby with wispy brown hair! Another mother is seen, with another baby. The figs are everywhere and they relish them. Other orang-utans appear: as many adults as possible, and if not many then the two babies are adorable, at least. They chew figs and play. After a time, they hear something and they hide. Oona finishes her journey and Will wakes.

Will Wow, there's a feast of figs here!

He gets off Oona and eats.

Why aren't you stuffing your face? What is it? Let it be the tiger!

Taking his cue from Oona, he is on guard. Shaking of branches, rustling of leaves. Mani is seen.

Oh, hello, it's you again. I haven't seen you for weeks –

The orang-utans gingerly return to their feast. When Will moves they become agitated.

It's all right. I'm not going to hurt you. I promise.

Oona goes off to eat in the distance. Will cautiously picks up a fig and eats.

See. I'm your friend.

The orang-utans suckle, scratch, eat, play, yawn. Some appear to be showing off. Will laughs. Some move closer to Will. Suddenly they all seem to be approaching him.

Hey . . . what is this?

Mani's baby comes close to Will. Mani watches.

Look at you, then . . .

The baby touches his hand, tentatively. She grasps his finger and tugs it. She puts his finger on her face. She takes his ear.

Hey. That's my ear. And that's yours. We're sort of the same . . . We've both got hair, though mine's not red. And we've got hands, feet . . . You're a bit human and . . . I'm a bit animal. Tiny thing. What's your name, then? . . . You remind me of an old friend of mine called Charlie. He's pretty tiny. But maybe you're a girl. Oh, yes. I think you probably are. Sorry, Charlie in Salisbury.

The second baby screeches and makes a scene.

Oh, but you, you're definitely a Chelsea supporter and your name is Tonk. (*Re Mani, to 'Charlie'.*) Is that your mum? She's been following me. I can't think of a name for her . . .

He laughs, they play. He feeds 'Charlie'. A beautiful bird appears.

It's like a family, Oona.

And suddenly . . .

SCENE FIFTEEN
THE HUNTERS

Oona stampedes through the paradise, trumpeting. The bird flies off. A pick-up truck might career into the forest.

Voices in Indonesian: 'There, there!' Chaos. The orang-utans panic.

Will What –? No! Stop! Oona, come back! Oona, Oona!

Rifle-wielding hunters – one of them wearing a red bandana – fire.

Red Bandana (*in English*) Watch the babies!

Orang-utans swing wildly in the trees. 'Charlie' swings back to Mani. Mani is hit. 'Charlie' is on her own. Shots. Adult orang-utans fall.

Will Don't shoot! Stop shooting! Stop!

A Hunter (*in Indonesian*) A boy, a boy!

Will is caught. During the following, surviving orang-utans scarper, though not the two babies, 'Charlie' and 'Tonk', who are captured by the Hunters.

Red Bandana (*in Indonesian, to Will*) Who are you? (*To hunters.*) The babies!

Will Don't shoot, please!

Red Bandana (*in English*) English?

Will Charlie!

Red Bandana What are you doing here?

A Hunter (*in Indonesian*) A boy out here?

Red Bandana (*in English*) Who the hell are you?

A Hunter (*in Indonesian*) What are we going to do with him?

Red Bandana (*in Indonesian*) Put him in the truck with the orang-utans.

Will Oona! Oona!

Red Bandana (*in English, to Will*) You're coming with us!

*A hunter accidentally or defensively shoots a baby orang-
utan (not 'Charlie' or 'Tonk'). Another baby manages
to escape.*

(*In English, to Hunter.*) Idiot! (*To Will.*) Lucky you're not
dead.

Hunter (*in English*) Better if he was.

Red Bandana (*to Hunters, in English, re 'Charlie' and
'Tonk'*) Get the babies.

*Hunters force Will and the screeching 'Charlie' and
'Tonk' into the back of the pick-up truck.*

Will (*ad lib*) No! Let me go! Oona! Don't hurt them!
You can't do this! Oona! Oona!

Red Bandana (*in English*) Shut up, English! (*Re dead
baby, to Hunters.*) Don't tell the boss we lost two. We
keep hunting. It's not over till we've got a tiger.

They drive off.

Will Oona! Oona! Ooooooooona!

*They have gone. Eerie silence. Mani revives. She limps,
injured, crying for her baby. More gunshots. Mani
scrambles off as quickly as she is able. The Chorus
sings its Jungle Music to climax.*

35

Act Two

SCENE ONE
CAGED

*A house in a shanty town. A cage for animals. In the
nearby jungle, the Chorus are workers. The relentless,
discordant thuds and grunts of their labour. They are
seen all around, hacking into the trees with axes and
chainsaws, hauling, etc. Taunting, whistling and monkey
imitating from Red Bandana and Hunters as they drag
Will and the terrified 'Charlie' and 'Tonk' from the pick-
up truck towards the cage.*

Red Bandana (*in English*) Move, monkey boy! Move!

Hunters Monkey, monkey, monkey boy! (*Etc.*)

Red Bandana (*in Indonesian*) Get them in the cage – the
boy as well.

Will (*overlapping*) No! Let go! Get off! Charlie!
Murderers! (*Etc., ad lib.*)

*Other Hunters follow with the tiger – it is now bloody
and dead, with her/his paws lashed to a long stick,
from which s/he hangs. More hunters arrive from the
house to help with the bounty. Will, 'Charlie' and
'Tonk' are forced into the cage. The terrified orang-
utans cling to Will, pushing their faces into him. Will
glares as the hunters laugh and poke and rattle the
cage with sticks.*

Red Bandana (*in Indonesian, re the tiger*) Look at him!
(*In English.*) We saw him running along the river!

*He poses in front of the tiger; a hunter from the house
takes a photograph.*

(*In English.*) One bullet straight between the eyes.

He fires a celebratory gunshot into the air.

Hunter from the House (*in English*) The boss'll be pleased.

Will Murderers!

Hunter from the House (*in Indonesian*) Who is he?

Red Bandana (*in English*) Him? He's just a monkey boy.

Will How could you, how could you!

Red Bandana (*in English*) Shut up. (*To hunters.*) I'll ring the boss. (*In Indonesian.*) We'll be getting drunk tonight.

All disperse to bully the workers. The workers' shift winds down.

Will How could they do this? What is this place?

The distressed orang-utans suck on Will's fingers.

I know, Charlie, you've lost your mum. I know what that's like. We'll think of something. Shhh . . . it's all right . . . Oona will come for us . . .

He rocks himself and the orang-utans to sleep as the workers' shift ends and all rest.

SCENE TWO
KAYA

Kaya appears, holding a bucket. He goes to Will's cage and wakes him.

Kaya Hello? Wake up, boy.

He looks about, then cautiously takes a bottle of water from the bucket.

Drink.

He forces the bottle on Will. The orang-utans wake and scramble about, agitated.

Better?

Will You speak English?

Kaya Here. Durian. Fruit. It smells bad, but tastes good. I'm Kaya. Chef. Kaya's your friend.

Will I don't have any friends. None that are human, anyway.

Kaya It's not just for you, boy, it's for them too. Shhh, give me that.

He means the water bottle, which he hides. Red Bandana appears, holding his rifle.

Red Bandana (*in Indonesian*) You feeding them?

Kaya (*in English*) You know they only want food from their mother.

Red Bandana (*in English*) They look hungry. If they're not fed before Mr Anthony gets here, I'll beat you to hell. None for Monkey Boy, he starves.

He leaves.

Kaya It's the same thing every time hunters steal orang-utans from the jungle: 'feed babies'. They want to keep them alive, but only because no one buys dead baby orang-utans. But this young they don't like to take food from strangers, so it's impossible.

Will They murdered their mothers.

Kaya If you feed them, I'll give you more water.

Will So they're going to sell them?

Kaya If they live. They might die. But not from starvation.

Will Then from what?

Kaya Sadness. And I get beaten. You want more to drink? Do it.

Will feeds 'Charlie' and 'Tonk'. During the next they cautiously eat the fruit.

You're a wild monkey boy of the forest? Is it true? Everyone says so.

Will I suppose. There was a wave, and –

Kaya The *tsunami*? You've been out there all that time?

Will An elephant saved me. Called Oona.

Kaya An elephant saved you. Called Oona.

Will It's true.

Kaya Well, stranger things have happened – for example, you make a very good orang-utan mother. They're eating – Thank you – I won't get hit.

Will My name's Will.

Kaya You like coconut, Will?

Will nods. Kaya gives him pieces of coconut from his pockets.

Will How can you work here? Look what they did to the tiger.

Kaya I have to make money for my family. I have a grandson your age. We all have to live. I don't like it, but if I say what I think, they'll send me away or worse; they could kill me. These aren't good people, they do bad things.

Will What will they do with me?

Kaya They won't decide, Mr Anthony will decide.

Will Mr Anthony?

Kaya From Jakarta, my boss, everyone's boss. See: he's stripped the whole valley. The *tsunami* made things worse for some people – and better for Mr Anthony. He's like God around here. Your babies are happier. Shhh!

A helicopter is heard.

Already? I have to go.

Will But, Kaya –

Kaya Don't tell them I helped you –

Red Bandana appears.

Red Bandana (*in Indonesian*) Hurry!

The Hunters assemble and . . .

SCENE THREE
MR ANTHONY

Black-suited bodyguards enter, carrying rifles. They are followed by Mr Anthony. He wears his hair slicked and has white trousers, polished shoes, gold rings and dark glasses. Workers and Kaya attend his every need. He inspects the tiger.

Mr Anthony Stunning. (*To Red Bandana.*) Well done.

He looks to the cage. Kaya gives him a drink, a plate of food, etc.

And you. So it's true. A real-life monkey boy. How did you get here? Tourist? You even got a name?

Will I'm not telling you my name.

Mr Anthony Now don't be a nuisance, I don't like nuisances. (*Re food.*) This is disgusting, Kaya: salt.

Kaya rushes off with the plate of food.

Will How could you kill a tiger? Why?

Mr Anthony Why? 'Cause tigers make lovely tiger *skins*. 'Cause rich people like fancy rugs. They pay me ten thousand bucks for this in California. And those little orang-utans? Five thousand a head. People in Jakarta love them as pets for their kids. Businessmen, my mates in the police, politicians; I sell, they buy. Money, Monkey Boy. Money is power. And I'm the richest man you'll ever meet. The real question is: what's the worth of *you*?

Kaya rushes back on with Mr Anthony's salted food.

Say hello to Monkey Boy, Kaya.

Kaya Hello.

Mr Anthony Say, 'Hello, Monkey Boy'.

Kaya Hello, Monkey Boy.

Mr Anthony (*to Will*) See: everyone here does what I tell them.

Will Not me. Let us back to the jungle!

Mr Anthony But the jungle is *mine*. And unless you're working for me, you're trespassing. So are you gonna work? All the trees need flattening. I need ruddy great bonfires made of the whole forest. And I need *new* trees planted, better trees, quick-growers. Kaya, tell Monkey Boy what this was cooked in.

Kaya Cooking oil, Mr Anthony.

Mr Anthony Tell him where the cooking oil comes from.

Kaya Palm trees.

Mr Anthony You like chips, Monkey Boy? Palm oil. Biscuits? Palm oil. Toothpaste, peanut-butter, soap, shampoo – the whole world's screaming for palm oil! So, how about you work for me so your mates in England can have lots of lovely things?

Will Burn the jungle? The jungle's home to animals.

Mr Anthony Animals?

Laughter.

What about *people*? People need jobs and food and houses. I give them a life – *palm trees* give them a life.

Will You're a poacher and a murderer – you're the devil!

Mr Anthony You don't get it, do you? I'm giving you a chance. You think you can live on my patch *and not be of value to me*? So you won't work? Then what am I going to do with you? I know! I'll sell you to the circus. There are circuses all over India I've sold orang-utans to, why not a boy? 'Presenting the all-singing, all-dancing Monkey Boy!' You can dance, right? So, dance. Sing. I said sing, orphan boy. Do it.

Hunters Do it, do it, do it . . .

Taunting, monkey noises. Mr Anthony grabs a rifle from a bodyguard.

Mr Anthony Sing, or I'll kill those baby orang-utans under your nose and feed them to my dogs.

Will
Glory, glory, Man United,
Glory, glory, Man United,
Glory, glory, Man United,
As the Reds go marching
On. On. On.

Mr Anthony There. Now you see how it works here. You dance to my tune. Just like Kaya and everyone here. (*Re tiger.*) And aren't you the jackpot?

He begins to walk off.

Will
　　Tyger Tyger, burning bright –

Mr Anthony looks back at him. Will recites bravely,
unflinching.

In the forests of the night;
What immortal hand or eye,
Dare frame thy fearful symmetry?

Tyger, tyger, burning bright,
Burning bright,
Burning bright.

A moment. All stare at Mr Anthony.

Mr Anthony You know, I have this feeling the only thing
I'm gonna get out of you is pleasure from –

He pantomimes a bullet to the head.

(*To hunters.*) We drink.

He begins a drinking song and the Hunters join in.
Bottles are distributed. Will, 'Charlie' and 'Tonk' are
terrorised and . . .

SCENE FOUR
ESCAPE

The Hunters are drunk. Their songs are heard in the
distance. Red Bandana approaches the cage, drinking and
drunk. He taunts.

Red Bandana 'Glory, glory, Man United . . .'

Will I need water.

Red Bandana 'I need water.'

He stumbles off. 'Charlie' and 'Tonk' are agitated.

Will I know . . . Shhh . . . I know . . .

Kaya carefully avoids hunters and makes it to the cage, carrying his bucket.

Kaya, I'm dying of thirst –

Kaya No time. It's against the law to poach. They hate you because you've seen their faces, and I really think he could kill you. Hear their party? Your chance.

Will Have you got keys?!

Kaya There's more than one way to skin a rabbit.

He produces kitchen implements from his bucket and picks the lock to the cage.

I like the tiger poem you spoke. I learnt it in my mission school a long time ago – it stayed in my head.

Will I don't know why I said it.

Kaya It was all you had. Who is it by, I forget?

Will Blake. I don't remember all of it.

Kaya You remember enough to – how you say – rattle Mr Anthony's cage. One day you have to tell the world who they are and they'll go to prison for a long time.

Will Stop!

He has seen Mr Anthony come out of the house with a set of keys. Kaya feeds 'Charlie' and 'Tonk' from his bucket.

Mr Anthony What are you doing?

Kaya Feeding them, Mr Anthony . . . they're eating properly at last.

Mr Anthony Just off to the gun-house . . . I need the right weapon for the purpose . . .

He walks off.

Kaya Hurry!

The cage is opened.

Will He'll know you did it!

Kaya I don't care. Before your tiger poem, I was afraid, then I saw Mr Anthony frightened of a boy and I'm not afraid any more.

Will I don't know where I am!

Kaya The jungle's that way –

Will Then what do I do?!

Kaya You're a wild boy, you know how to hide out there.

Will But I had Oona before –

Kaya So find Oona.

Will Thank you, Kaya.

Kaya Whenever I say 'Tyger Tyger' I'll remember you. Go, go fast!

Hounds bark. Kaya rushes off. Will escapes into the night, carrying 'Charlie' and pulling 'Tonk' by the hand. Mr Anthony returns. He has a pistol. He sees the empty cage. He roars.

Mr Anthony Where is he?!

Hunters stagger in from their party.

My patch, Monkey Boy! My trees, my river, my tigers, my orang-utans! I hunt: I burn: I reap the palm trees that I sow. I. Am. God! GOD!

The hunters tear after Will, wielding guns and machetes, whistling, etc. Shouts ad lib:

Red Bandana Spread out!

45

Hunters (*in Indonesian*) He knows who we are! That way, the jungle! Get him, after him!

Mr Anthony pursues Kaya with the pistol.

Mr Anthony Kaya. Kaya.

And . . .

SCENE FIVE
BACK TO THE RAINFOREST

Will, 'Charlie' and 'Tonk' run for their lives towards – and through – the rainforest, pursued by hunters and their hounds.

Chorus (*as required*)
  – The night, the track,
  – the hill, the mud,
  – mile after mile,
  – *the screams,
  – brain fogs, eyes blur,
  – mouth burns, ears whir
  – the forest, the forest,
  – *the rainforest.

Will, 'Charlie' and 'Tonk' stop running, exhausted, still fearful.

Will We'll rest here . . . I'll find Oona . . . Oona?

He's frightened, but dares to call a little louder, and finally very loud:

Oona? How am I going to find you? Ooooonaaaa!

And . . .

SCENE SIX
THE TREEHOUSE

Hunters call – 'There! That way!' – then gunshots. The Jungle Music, panicky. Terror: 'Charlie' and 'Tonk' cling to Will, chittering. He looks around. There's nothing for it but to climb a tree. As they head towards the canopy, hunters appear below them, many more than we've seen, a phalanx. The jungle is silent as they traverse the landscape, holding rifles, slashing through undergrowth with machetes. One has a dead adult orang-utan over his shoulders. They disappear but Red Bandana stops, sensing something. He is at the base of Will's tree. Will puts his head in the orang-utans' hair, willing them to be quiet. Red Bandana taunts.

Red Bandana Where are you, Monkey Boy? I'll find you. And every orang-utan I see on the way gets one in the head. I serve Mr Anthony, and he wants you dead. Monkey, Monkey, Monkey Boy . . . 'Glory, glory, Man United . . .'

He moves on and disappears.

Will I think we're safe here . . . there's fruit in these trees . . . We'll just take each day as it comes . . . like Oona taught me.

He puts his head in his hands.

Chill, Will; chill, Will; chill, Will . . .

'Charlie' prises Will's hands away from his face and touches him.

Hello. Sorry. I'm missing Oona, that's all. Like you miss your mum.

'Charlie' kisses him on the nose.

Hey. What's that, then? Charlie, you soppy bugger. What will we do without her? I don't even know why I rely on her . . . Flies hover round her bum and she farts non-stop and basically she's just on the planet to stuff her face . . . But she's my friend. Like you. You speak with your eyes, just like her.

'Charlie' sits on his shoulders and delves into his hair with her fingers, grooming him.

Why would Mr Anthony want to kill your mother and kidnap you – you wouldn't hurt a fly. It's only humans who kill for greed or the fun of it.

'Tonk' stops what he's doing and tries to push 'Charlie' away from Will.

All right, Tonk, I haven't forgotten you, I love you too.

'Tonk' does something clever, something imitative.

Hey, you clever boy! Kaya was right, I'm like your mother. You know, I'm not sure I'll ever see the real Charlie and Tonk again. All that matters is we stay alive and find Oona. This jungle's ginormous – but she's here looking for me, I have to keep believing that.

'Charlie' and 'Tonk' gambol about – more than that, they swing in the trees in ways we haven't seen thus far. They are growing up before Will's eyes. And . . .

SCENE SEVEN
THE JUNGLE BALLET

The jungle of the air comes to life. Howling and hooting. Amazingly, if possible, new creatures we haven't seen: gibbons and/or monkeys, bats and colourful birds. They swing and fly from branch to branch. It's a whole new

world above the ground, and it's wondrous. Will is
awestruck – and envious.

Will Tonk? Charlie! Where are you going?

An orang-utan – Mani – makes her way towards
'Charlie' and . . .

SCENE EIGHT
MANI'S RETURN

Charlie is very curious and clambers all over Mani. Will
doesn't realise who it is at first. 'Tonk' scampers to Mani
as well. The Jungle Music, sweet and seductive. Mum and
Dad appear, hand in hand.

Will Dear Mum and Dad. Today we walked for miles . . .

Mum 'Today we walked for miles, the humidity's
disgusting, the leeches are drinking me to death, I hear
poachers all the time and I think I've lost Oona for ever.'

Dad 'But just when I thought I couldn't do it any more,
we came across this orang-utan with a scar on her
shoulder . . .'

Will watches the orang-utans as they bond.

Mum 'She's so tender with them, especially Charlie. And
then the most incredible thing happened . . .'

Mani lets 'Charlie' suckle her. Will laughs, amazed.

Will Wow . . . it's your mum, Charlie. She's alive!

Dad 'I know it's stupid, but I sort of felt like I'd been
brushed aside . . .'

Mum 'Then this morning . . .'

Mani brings 'Charlie' and 'Tonk' towards Will. She
reaches and touches his hand.

Will That's crazy. You can't be thanking me. That's crazy.

Mum 'Anyway . . . that's what I'd write to you, if I could.'

Will Love, Will.

She and Dad disappear. Suddenly: Oona's trumpeting is heard. Smoke.

Oona?

He descends the tree hurriedly and . . .

SCENE NINE
FIRE

Oona charges out of the trees and heads for Will. He's elated, hugs her trunk, etc., but she is troubled.

Will Oona! Oona, at last, what took you so long? I knew you'd find me, oh, I've missed you, I love you, every pink bit of you, every smelly inch, where have you been, where –?

Oona keeps trumpeting. Mani, 'Charlie' and 'Tonk' come down from the tree, chittering and calling.

All right, it's me, what's the matter with you?

He only wants to hug Oona but she keeps trumpeting. The whole jungle whoops and caws and screeches. Every single forest creature is on the move. The smoke thickens.

What's happening?

Oona trumpets. Mani rushes past Will with 'Charlie' and 'Tonk' as if urging Will to follow in a particular direction.

No-name, where are you going? No-name!

Oona trumpets as she kneels. Will coughs and splutters.

Fire? Fire!

He panics. The smoke is everywhere. Will climbs on to Oona with difficulty. Oona follows Mani, 'Charlie' and 'Tonk'. Hunters are everywhere, vengeful brutes in the shadows. Thick and ugly smoke. Gunshots, torchlight, flames. Shouts in Indonesian and English – 'Get the English boy!', 'Dead or alive!', 'That way!', 'Shoot him on sight!', 'Burn!', 'He knows who we are!', 'We're coming for you, Monkey, Monkey, Monkey Boy!'. Whoops and caws and screeches and . . .

SCENE TEN
TO THE SANCTUARY

Will and Oona, led by Mani, 'Charlie' and 'Tonk', run off, pursued by the hunters and the fire. The smoke chokes Will. Mr Anthony's voice is heard booming after them through the forest, through a loud-hailer.

Mr Anthony's Voice I burn forest! I make a ruddy great bonfire to clear the ancient trees to plant the palms to make the palm oil to grow rich! –

Will Oona . . . stop . . . Are you following her? . . . No-name, where are you going! No-name!

Mr Anthony's Voice I'll smoke you out, Monkey Boy!

Will Stop . . . please, stop . . .

Mr Anthony's Voice This is my patch! –

Will Oona . . . I can't breathe . . .

Mr Anthony's Voice I'm God!

51

Mani has led Will and Oona to a river; it rushes and gushes noisily; the current is immense. The Chorus sings. Mani won't stop, and begins to cross, heading for an island on the other side, risking the lives of 'Charlie' and 'Tonk'. Oona follows, and it's all Will can do to stay on her back. He is sick, exhausted, his lungs full of smoke, then water. The river is as powerful and destructive as the tsunami.

Mr Anthony is seen, with a rifle. His voice is heard again, disconnected from his body.

Mr Anthony's Voice I'm God. I. AM. GOD.

He fires. The bang echoes. Will is hit in the shoulder and he falls and the water swallows him. Mani, 'Charlie' and 'Tonk' make it to the shore of the island.

The Chorus sings a lullaby as Will, bloody and seemingly dead, is washed to the shore. The Chorus are women, who rush towards him with a stretcher. One of them is Dr Geraldine, who wears a tatty straw hat. Will is lifted on to the stretcher, and taken away. Oona follows. Dr Geraldine takes Mani's hand. And . . .

SCENE ELEVEN
BUFFOONERY OF BABY ORANG-UTANS

Baby Orang-utans are everywhere, more than we've seen, twenty if possible. Some wear nappies! The women – foster mothers – nurse them, feeding them from bottles. Rolling, clambering, sleeping, feeding, fighting, playing: a magical sight: a Buffoonery of Baby Orang-utans. And . . .

Will is asleep on a camp-bed outside a hut, his shoulder bandaged. Dr Geraldine sits by his bedside with a book. Oona is nearby. Mani is here; she watches as 'Charlie' and 'Tonk' gambol about. As the Chorus's lullaby finishes we hear Dr Geraldine reading 'The Elephant's Child'.

Dr Geraldine '. . . Then the Elephant's Child sat back on his little paunches, and pulled, and pulled, and pulled, and his nose began to stretch . . .'

Will wakes.

Will Mum?

Dr Geraldine You're awake –?

Will Mum, you're alive . . .

Dr Geraldine I'm not your mother . . . my name's Geraldine . . .

Will clings to her, whispering over and over, 'Mum, Mum'.

Shhh . . . it's all right . . . you've got colour in your cheeks at last . . . (*To a foster mother, sotto.*) Tell them – tell everyone he's awake –

The foster mother leaves.

Will You survived it, I found you –

Dr Geraldine Listen to me. I'm not your mother, see?

Will – only you know how much I love that story.

Dr Geraldine Look at me. I'm not her. Understand?

Will stares at her, and nods.

I'm Geraldine.

Oona searches Will with her trunk.

Will Oona? Oona! You're alive . . . good girl . . . you didn't die . . .

He hugs her.

Dr Geraldine She hasn't left you for a second. We tried to move her to feed her, but she wouldn't budge – so the food was brought to you, wasn't it, your majesty?

Will Oona, we're never leaving each other again, *ever* . . .

Dr Geraldine She saved your life. Well, her and Mani.

Will Mani?

Dr Geraldine indicates Mani.

(*To Mani.*) You? . . . You're here too?

Dr Geraldine A very old friend of mine.

'Charlie' and 'Tonk' and other Orang-utans scamper towards Will.

Will Hello, Charlie! Tonk! I've missed you, Charlie!

Dr Geraldine Careful of your shoulder – you were hurt badly, and you've been very sick, smoke inhalation. It was touch and go for a while.

Will Charlie . . .

Dr Geraldine That's a good name . . . you do realise she's a girl?

Will (*nods*) Are we . . . on an island?

Dr Geraldine Yes. My orphanage. For animals, not children. Orang-utans I'm used to; boys from England, not so much.

Will Orphanage?

Dr Geraldine All these babies have lost their mothers. Mani lost hers. She was someone's caged pet once – then

54

she was rescued and came to me. Now she's wild again. But it doesn't stop her from coming back to visit sometimes.

Will (*trying to recall things*) I think Oona might have followed her here . . .

Dr Geraldine Yes, she's clever.

Will There was smoke . . . a fire and . . . the poachers wanted to kill us –

Dr Geraldine You were shot.

Will – and the current was so strong and . . . I don't remember . . . just you reading . . . and Oona farting and farting and farting.

He looks about in amazement at the orang-utans in nappies.

How long have you lived here?

Dr Geraldine A long time. I call it my 'university of the jungle'. These women from the villages live here and help me. When orang-utans like Charlie graduate, they go back to where they belong – but with half a chance of fending off their predators.

Will Why do people want to hurt them?

Dr Geraldine You were chased by poachers, weren't you?

Will Yes.

Dr Geraldine Then you know why. They're safe here. And so are you.

Will We're safe, Oona . . . It's peaceful . . . and beautiful. (*To Dr Geraldine.*) I know, Oona and I can help you!

Dr Geraldine All that matters now is that you rest and eat.

Will But we're a team, and I've got nowhere else to go – and we can't let those murderers win!

Dr Geraldine True, Will, we can't.

Will is confused.

Will How do you know my name? . . . and how did you know 'The Elephant's Child' was my favourite story?

Dr Geraldine You've been through so much. I know you've got lots of questions, but the important thing is you get strong.

Granny and Grandad enter.

Granny Will? Will . . .

She hugs him. Grandad holds back, taciturn as always.

Will Granny?

Granny You've been so sick . . . you poor boy . . .

Grandad Will . . .

Will Grandad . . .

He gives in to his emotions and hugs them.

Grandad I always knew you were alive . . .

Granny It's all thanks to Dr Geraldine. We came to the island months ago, we were searching for you all along the river, dropping leaflets in every town. We didn't hear from anybody, then out of the blue two weeks ago she rang us and said she'd found you.

Grandad Look at you. You're a man now. (*For Lilly:* 'You're all grown-up.')

A moment.

Will? Your (*mother*) –

Will No. No, don't say anything.

He walks away a little, towards Oona.

I know Mum drowned. I know that. I always knew.

He whispers to Oona.

Grandad Oona.

Will You know her name?

Dr Geraldine You kept calling for her in your dreams . . .

Grandad This is the girl who kept us going. Wherever we went, we kept hearing the same story about a beach elephant who took a boy off into the jungle.

Granny Now . . . you don't need to worry about a thing. You'll come and live with us in Yorkshire – like you always wanted. We need another pair of hands on the farm. And you'll go to St Paul's Primary and you'll make lots of new friends . . .

Grandad Leave him be . . .

Will Yorkshire? But you're the one who wanted me to come to Indonesia. You bought the tickets.

Granny Yes . . . it's my fault . . .

Will No, I didn't mean that . . . The wave killed Mum, not you . . . but how can I go back to Yorkshire now?

Granny It's where we're from . . . It's where your dad grew up. It's home.

Dr Geraldine Let's all go and have something to eat . . .

But Will won't leave Oona.

Granny It'll be a good life. We're going home, Will.

Dr Geraldine guides Granny into the hut.

Grandad Join us when you want to.

He follows Granny. The orang-utans play. And . . .

SCENE THIRTEEN
WILL'S FAMILY

Will is with Oona, Mani nearby. 'Charlie' and 'Tonk' are with foster mothers. Dr Geraldine appears from the hut. Will doesn't notice her at first. He sings to Oona. She is restless.

Will
Glory, glory, Will and Oona,
Glory, glory, Will and Oona,
Glory, glory, Will and Oona,
Will and Oona running wild . . .

Mani approaches.

Hello, Mani.

Dr Geraldine All packed?

Will I don't own anything.

Dr Geraldine Your grandparents are just coming.

Will Oona's not eating this morning. She knows.

Dr Geraldine I'm sorry I didn't get a chance to ride on her before you left.

Will You could! We could go into the jungle now, the three of us.

Dr Geraldine gives him a book.

For you. Your grandad told me three generations of your family have read these stories.

Will When will Charlie and Tonk go back to the jungle?

Dr Geraldine Soon. The point is to persuade them not to rely on humans. I suppose we're like their mothers and fathers . . . but like all families on the one hand the

58

children need the parents, and on the other they don't
need them at all.

Will Will Oona forget me, Dr Geraldine?

Dr Geraldine Don't be silly, you know perfectly well that
an elephant never forgets.

*Charlie scampers to Dr Geraldine and removes her
hat. She is half bald beneath.*

Will Charlie . . .!

Dr Geraldine It's all right.

She laughs. Will retrieves her hat. He stares.

What, this? You make enemies doing our kind of work.
You know that yourself.

Will Hunters?

Dr Geraldine A present from one of the big boys in
Jakarta.

Will Mr Anthony?

Dr Geraldine I don't know his name –

*Grandad appears from the hut with a suitcase,
unnoticed.*

They can't stand us saving animals. One night they tried
to burn us out and my hair caught fire. I keep it under my
hat, so to speak.

Will So both of us were nearly killed by the big boys.

Dr Geraldine But they won't succeed, will they? They
can't stop us. We've saved lots of orang-utans but we're
going to have to save lots more – if we don't, then in five
years there'll be none left in the wild.

Will And nobody even realises.

Dr Geraldine Some people do.

Will Not where I'm from, they don't. People just want what they want. I didn't even know what palm oil was before I met Mani. In England, I remember seeing this picture online of a burnt rainforest. There was this petrified little orang-utan at the top of a burnt tree. I was probably stuffing my face with pizza or chips, and I didn't understand what it meant.

Dr Geraldine Well, you understand now. We make a good team, you and I. I'm glad you came.

Will I don't have to go. I could stay. I could help you.

Dr Geraldine I know you want to . . . I want you to, but . . . (*Re book.*) There are two bookmarks in here . . . This one . . . is the leaflet your grandparents gave me when they came searching for you. It shows how much they love you. The second bookmark is a prophecy of the Cree Native Americans. I live my life by it. Read it when you're on the plane.

Granny appears from the hut with her handbag and suitcase.

Granny We don't want to miss the boat.

She puts the suitcase down to hold her hand out to Dr Geraldine. 'Charlie' scampers towards the suitcase and during the next opens it and plays with the contents without Granny realising.

Thank you. There were some days when it was so hard . . . and your phone call was the best call of my life. We owe you so much.

Dr Geraldine You don't owe me anything . . .

Will Charlie!

He laughs and controls 'Charlie'. Granny sees the damage.

Granny Oh . . .

Will gathers up Granny's belongings – which include toiletries.

(*Continuing to Dr Geraldine.*) They're amazing creatures. What you do here is wonderful. We'll miss it . . .

Will Soap. Shampoo. These are the reasons, Granny.

Granny What?

Will This is why it's happening.

Granny I don't understand.

A moment.

Well. (*To Dr Geraldine.*) Will you come to the jetty?

Mani holds her hand out to Grandad, much as she once did to Will. He kneels and their heads touch. Grandma is taken aback.

What's she doing?

Dr Geraldine Thanking him.

Granny What for?

Dr Geraldine For Will.

A moment.

I won't come down, if you don't mind.

She quickly kisses Will goodbye.

Goodbye. I won't forget you. What you've done is extraordinary.

She exits into the hut, concealing her emotions. The foster mothers retreat with 'Charlie' and 'Tonk' and any other babies.

Granny Ready? Oona can follow. You can say goodbye down there. Come on, then.

She heads towards the jetty with her suitcase. Grandad follows her. Will follows him. Oona won't move. Will stops and turns back to Oona, caught between her and his grandparents.

Will Grandad . . .

Grandad and Granny stop.

Grandad It's all right . . . we have five minutes . . .

Granny Two minutes, we have two minutes.

She and Grandad leave. Will goes to Oona. During the next Grandad returns and watches.

Will Oona . . . I don't know why I have to do this, after everything . . . I love Granny and Grandad . . . but I haven't told them the half of it, and I don't think I'll ever be able to explain it or how much everything's changed. You're the only one who understands. Thank you for saving my life . . .

As he hugs her the second bookmark falls out of the book. He picks it up and reads it.

Chorus
  – 'When all the trees have been cut down,
  – when all the animals have been hunted,
  – when all the waters are polluted,
  – when all the air is unsafe to breathe,
  – only then will you discover you cannot eat money.'

Will kisses Oona and runs in the direction of Grandad, overwhelmed. Suddenly, he stops in his tracks. He doesn't turn. The Chorus sings. Behind Will, Oona kneels for him.

Grandad You have an invitation.

Will turns back towards Oona. He runs to her and climbs on her. Granny returns.

Will Top of the world . . .

Granny Will? Will! . . .

Dr Geraldine comes out of the hut.

Dr Geraldine You'll miss the boat . . .

Will I want to grow up to help Dr Geraldine.

Granny Come down . . .

Will England isn't my home any more. There has to be a way. You have to let me stay or promise to help find a way, because, because, because where there's a Will there's a way, right? Otherwise . . . otherwise, Granny and Grandad, you're going to lose me a second time. Promise me there's a way.

Grandad I promise . . .

Granny (*to Grandad*) Don't be silly. (*To Will.*) Grandad doesn't know what he's saying . . .

Grandad Grandad is saying . . . that his mum and dad would have been proud . . . and I promise to find a way.

'Charlie' bounds on naughtily, a foster mother in pursuit. She clings to Granny.

Granny Heavens. Hello again.

Will And maybe this is where you're meant to be as well! Because . . . the animals and the *tsunami* and Mum and the jungle, they've, I don't know, I haven't got the words, Granny . . .

Oona farts. Will laughs.

They've opened my eyes, and I'm tied to them now – because some people have to be. If I can save one more animal, I can save a whole world. I want to be Geraldine's eyes and ears in the jungle. It's where I belong. This is home. So run wild, Oona. Run wild!

They ride off. The Chorus sings joyfully. All the animals are seen.

The End.